T0147181

Answers *to* Faith *Crushing* Questions

BOB GREEN

WESTBOW
PRESS®
A DIVISION OF THOMAS NELSON
& ZONDERVAN

WestBow Press books may be ordered through booksellers or by contacting:

WestBow Press
A Division of Thomas Nelson & Zondervan
1663 Liberty Drive
Bloomington, IN 47403
www.westbowpress.com
844-714-3454

ISBN: 978-1-6642-5032-1 (sc)
ISBN: 978-1-6642-5033-8 (e)

Library of Congress Control Number: 2021924456

Print information available on the last page.

WestBow Press rev. date: 03/22/2022

Contents

Preface

The purpose of this book is to provide answers to difficult questions in life that I have encountered over the last fifty years. Too many times these questions were posed to destroy my faith or discredit God.

The Bible says, "My people are destroyed for lack of knowledge" (Hosea 4:6 New American Standard Bible). Too many skeptics try to destroy the faith of others by asking difficult questions that seek to seed doubt and disbelief into a person's faith. Jesus ran into this frequently from both religious and nonreligious persons. His poignant answers very quickly ended the faith-busting derisions.

I hope these answers remove any doubts others have sought to hurt you with.

It has been alleged that Mark Twain said to a client after writing a book: "Madam, enclosed is the novel you commissioned in two volumes; if I had more time, I could have written it in one!" I have taken that extra time to hone these issues down to their essence. Please feel free to contact me with any comments or questions.

Book Cover

The painting is in the ceiling of the Sistine Chapel in the Vatican in Rome painted by Michaelangelo, 1508-1512. It depicts a helpless mankind being saved from himself by the pro-active, loving God.

For more information, please see our website:
FaithCrushingQuestions.com

Contact Bob at:
bob@faithcrushingquestions.com

Acknowledgments

My thanks to friends who proofread the manuscript. God bless you.

Bible versions used for this book are:
New International Version (NIV)
King James Version (KJV)
New King James Version (NKJV)
New American Standard Bible (NASB)
New Living Translation (NLT)
Good News Translation (GNT)
Berean Study Bible (BSB)

1

What Are Your Presuppositions?

Whenever we enter a discussion on any topic, whether it be political, religious, philosophical, life issues, etc., our positions are based on presuppositions. These presuppositions are beliefs, values, doctrines, philosophies, experiences that we have acquired over time that become the basis of our opinions and positions on matters.

These presuppositions can also be called our worldview. It is a summary of what we believe and know about the world around us. These beliefs, values, perspectives, and experiences are accumulated over time starting in childhood watching and listening to our parents, relatives, neighbors, friends, teachers, schools, clubs, the culture and society into which we are born.

Yet even with all this input, we are still limited to knowing just the world around us. We as finite beings cannot know what is beyond the experiences of this world unless it is revealed to us. For example, if extraterrestrials revealed themselves to us, just think of the incredible knowledge of the universe and science they would teach us that we presently do not know and had no way of knowing.

Your presuppositions about the world you live in would change. It is the same with the knowledge of God.

2

How Can the Finite Know the Infinite?

In the Star Trek movie *Into Darkness*, First Officer Spock is planting a device in an active volcano to prevent it from destroying a planet. He succeeds, but to rescue Spock, Captain Kirk must violate the Prime Directive, (for you non-Trekkies: not interfering with the natural development of a civilization even if it is well intentioned). In this case that would happen by revealing the starship to a primitive people, who could see it fly and disappear into the heavens. But to save Spock, Captain Kirk has no choice but for the primitive peoples to see the starship. This revelation suddenly changes everything they know. It influences their development, the art they draw, etc.

As finite creatures, how are we able to know anything about the infinite unless the infinite reveals it to us? That is exactly what the Bible is. It is a collection of sixty-six books, written over a fifteen-hundred-year period by thirty-five to forty authors. We do not know for certain who wrote some of the books, like Job and Hebrews. Second Timothy 3:16 tells us these authors wrote under the inspiration of the Holy Spirit. That is why there is a common theme carried through all the books; there was just one author—God. Moses wrote the first five books. The Ten Commandments were written in stone by the hand of God directly. Apostle John wrote the last book, Revelation. These sixty-six books contain stories of God revealing Himself to men and women, boys and girls by being directly involved in their lives. God not only informs people about Himself; He helps people get through difficult and dangerous life situations and in the process reveals various aspects of Himself to them and to us.

For example, Moses grew up in the home of Pharaoh, the ruler in

Egypt. As a young man, when he saw the injustice of the task masters over his people and slew one of them, he fled into the desert and never wanted to go back again. The Lord intervened in his life, calling him back to Egypt some fifty years later when he was eighty, into a conflict with the most powerful of all Egypt's pharaohs; Ramses II. Cecil B. DeMille's epic film *The Ten Commandments* employed two of the best actors in Hollywood, Charlton Heston as Moses, and Yul Brynner as Pharaoh, to visually portray this titanic struggle for the freedom of a whole race of people from slavery. Through this live interaction and intervention, God broke the yoke of slavery binding the Hebrew people using a hesitant Moses who had failed when he tried it on his own decades earlier. As a result, the Hebrew people at the time, and now we also, learn much about the character, holiness, justice, mercy, and power of almighty God as He vanquishes the power of the gods of Egypt and of Pharaoh, the mightiest empire in that region at that time.

The same is true with the numerous other real-life people God worked through, throughout the centuries. The Bible is a progressive revelation of God to us, by working through flawed and weak people just like us, since 1500 BC. This divine intervention in human history culminated in the life of Jesus, whose name is Emmanuel, which means God with us.

In addition, the last two thousand years of human history after Jesus is replete with the Lord's intervention into the lives of individuals, from kings like historical figures such as Constantine, philosophers such as Saint Augustine, and artists such as Michelangelo, whose vivid paintings on the wall and ceilings of the Sistine Chapel tell us much about our creator. The ceiling portrays an active God reaching out to save a helpless humankind that cannot save itself.

Scientists like Galileo, Newton, and Einstein, et al. understood there had to be an intelligent creator behind the creation.

For example, Sir Isaac Newton, the father of modern physics, said:

> *And from true lordship it follows that the true God is living, intelligent, and powerful; from the other perfections, that he is supreme, or supremely perfect.*

He is eternal and infinite, omnipotent and omniscient;
that is, he endures from eternity to eternity; and he is
present from infinity to infinity; he rules all things,
and he knows all things that happen or can happen.

Galileo said:

The prohibition of science would be contrary to
the Bible, which in hundreds of places teaches us
how the greatness and the glory of God shine forth
marvelously in all His works, and is to be read above
all in the open book of the heavens.

There are similar quotes from Kepler, Copernicus, et al.

Dr. Albert Einstein wanted to know God's thoughts as He created the world. He admired the illimitable superior spirit who reveals Himself in the slightest of scientific details that our frail and feeble minds can perceive. He believed everyone seriously involved in science becomes convinced of a spirit manifest in the laws of the universe vastly superior to human.

As with many modern scientists today, Einstein believed that science without religion is lame. Religion without science is blind.

The infinite God allows us to understand who He is, revealing His character and purpose in His creation, through the lives of hundreds of people, over fifteen hundred years, in His life manual to us—the Bible. If you follow the maintenance manual in your car, it will run correctly for years. If we follow the Creator's life manual for us—the Bible—we will better comprehend the world around us and be able to have a personal relationship with our creator because He has revealed Himself to us in the Bible, His written word. This revelation of the written word culminated in the coming of Jesus, who is called Emmanuel, God with us, and the Logos, the living word of God. (John 1). What better way to learn about the infinite than by following the creator of the universe, Jesus, in our lives (Colossians 1:16 New Living Translation).

3

God Is Good, So Why Is There Evil?

After God created the laws of physics, thermodynamics, mathematics, chemistry, biology, and all the other sciences, He then created the Universe with its billions of galaxies and innumerable life-forms. But He was not satisfied. He wanted to create something even better, grander, almost impossible, and even more wonderful. He wanted to create *you*! He wanted to create *us*! In Genesis 1:26 (New King James Version) God said, "Let Us make man in Our image, according to Our likeness." You could write a book on all this means. If God were an all-encompassing oneness of the universe, or an energy field, He would have made us that. Instead, He made us personal, living, spiritual beings because that is what He is.

One of the many ways God uses to describe Himself in the Bible is "I AM." The personal pronoun I, and the verb to be "am" describing a state of being or living existence. Therefore, since He is a personal, living being, He made us personal, living beings since we are made in "His image." He decided He wanted to create a living being like Himself, not just some impersonal force field of energy, of which the rest of the universe contains plenty. God is a spirit being, so He wanted a spirit being that would live eternally in fellowship with Him. A being like Himself with self-awareness and volition—freedom of independent choice not controlled in any way. A being like Himself, with the capacity to create the beauty of art and wisdom of science. A rational, intelligent being, with feelings and self-awareness. A being with a holy and righteous character as He has. But most amazingly, He wanted a being with the capacity, like Himself, to *love!* A being He could love and would love Him back.

Of course, love already existed, since most people would say that

God is love. But this time He wanted to create a spiritual/physical being with the capacity to love on its own volition—its own choice, not because it had to but because it wanted to. But to enable love in its most unfettered, purest form, He had to take a great risk. He had to first create free will. Unless love is entirely voluntary, an act of the will of a free moral agent, with no puppet strings attached, it is not love. If you program a robot to love you, that is not love, it is just a program running its course. Creating free will was risky because for there to be love, there must be the choice not to love. Indeed, even a choice to hate. For a being to love, God had to take a chance that it would not love Him or the other beings around it. Indeed, it would be free to hate Him and its fellow beings. If God forced this new being to love Him, then that response would not be love, just submission as a king or dictator could require of subjects. Apparently, the divine Creator decided a universe with beings that could choose to love was worth the risk of all the potential downsides.

Free will means the freedom of humans to make voluntary, personal choices that are not determined by prior causes or by divine intervention. Synonyms are self-motivated, uncoerced, unforced, volitional, voluntary, self-willing, self-determinate, and independent choice.

The story of this amazing creation of us starts in the first book of the Bible, at Genesis 1:27 et seq (New International Version):

> *So God created mankind in his own image, in the image of God he created them; male and female he created them.*

And continues in chapter 2:

> *Then the LORD God formed a man[c] from the dust of the ground and breathed into his nostrils the breath of life, and the man became a living being.*

> *Now the LORD God had planted a garden in the east, in Eden; and there he put the man he had formed.*

The LORD God made all kinds of trees grow out of the ground—trees that were pleasing to the eye and good for food. In the middle of the garden were the tree of life and the tree of the knowledge of good and evil. (Genesis 2:7–9)

The LORD God took the man and put him in the Garden of Eden to work it and take care of it. And the LORD God commanded the man, "You are free to eat from any tree in the garden; but you must not eat from the tree of the knowledge of good and evil, for when you eat from it you will certainly die." (Genesis 2:15–17)

Therefore, humankind was created in the image and likeness of God. That means we are intelligent, creative, have volition, are powerful especially today with nuclear weapons, have an eternal spirit, and have the capacity to love. We can love our Creator and the creation around us, just as the Creator does.

What a wonderful life our first parents had. Starting out with the top stewardship position to cultivate a beautiful tropical garden, all the free, fresh organic food you can eat, studying and naming the animals, living forever, and Adam running around with the exotic and stunning Eve all day, naked but not afraid as opposed to the TV show! Why? Because the Garden of Eden was made to be perfectly suited for their survival and comfort. Our first parents were given quite simple life instructions. Eat any of the fruit in the garden, including the tree of life to maintain eternal life, but do not partake of the tree of knowledge of good and evil. It was not an apple tree, by the way. We do not know if they were in Eden for a thousand years or ten minutes before they disobeyed. Many of us would have lasted just ten minutes in the Garden after running out of breath chasing Eve around and then going for the forbidden fruit! Remember as kids when we were told not to do something, many of us snuck around and did it anyway! So, we cannot put the blame on introducing evil into the world solely on our first parents. Be honest, eventually we all would have done the same act of disobedience if we had been in the Garden!

Freedom of Choice

At this point some would blame God for putting the tree of knowledge in the Garden in the first place. But that would have forced us into a forced, de facto obedience. We would have obeyed because we would not know there was an option not to obey. We would not have been presented with all of life's options, just a few preselected ones that would have produced a preselected outcome of perfect obedience. But that would not have been free will. For there to be love there must be a choice, a decision to love. Otherwise, it is not love—just a program running its prescribed course.

The First to Fall

The first to reject God's will was His most powerful, intelligent, and beautifully created being: the archangel Lucifer. Even his name is beautiful (*lucis*, light, and *fero*, to bring). In Latin, Light Bringer. Indeed, when he transformed into a serpent, even Eve takes notice of his beauty. Swelled with pride in all that he was, Lucifer purposed in his heart: "I will make myself like the Most High God" (Isaiah 14:14 New American Standard Bible). The creature wanted to supplant its creator. Indeed, he was followed in his rebellion by one third of the angels, who used their free will to rebel against God's love and authority. Humankind was next to fall, choosing to believe the devil's lie. "You will not certainly die," the serpent said to the woman. "For God knows that when you eat from it your eyes will be opened, and you will be like God, knowing good and evil." (Genesis 3:4–5 NASB) God did not say they were going to die immediately. But by willfully disobeying, they died first spiritually, severing their relationship with their Creator, and later they would die physically by being removed from the Garden where the Tree of Life was. The devil specializes in deceiving us even today using these kinds of half-truths.

Summary

Imagine, our first parents could have every beautiful thing the Garden had to offer, except that one fruit of the knowledge of good and evil. So, it was not God who introduced evil into the world; it was us—misusing our free will to do whatever we wanted, even if it defied our Maker's commands. We introduced evil into our own world and lives and have been struggling to control the evil inside our hearts ever since. We fell from grace, so we were removed from the Garden so we could not eat of the tree of life and live in rebellion to God's authority forever. We are under God's judgment. "It is destined for people to die once, and after this comes judgment" (Hebrews 9:27 NASB).

4

Consequences of Our Fall

Ever since then, we have all chosen to go our own way in life, too often ignoring God and His will for our lives. The Bible calls this "sin," which means to miss the mark, the mark of God's righteousness. Paradoxically, when we reject God's love, to find love on our own terms, we end up with lust or some other twisted, counterfeit version of the original. Claiming to be wise, we become fools because we become enslaved to our own self-centered passions, which ultimately leads to death. Sin is pleasurable for a season, but the way of it leads unto death. Not to mention disease, mental anguish, injury, psychological problems, and other negative consequences of wrong conduct.

Instead of using our free will to love and obey our Creator, we use it to pursue our own will. Imagine the sadness in the heart of God when His creation chooses not only not to love Him, but to actively defy His will in their lives.

Here is a short list of the ways humankind misuses free will compiled by the Apostle Paul in Romans 1:29–32 (NASB):

> People engage in: "Idolatry, immorality, sexual impurity, godlessness, suppression of the truth, every kind of wickedness, evil, greed and depravity. They are full of envy, murder, strife, deceit and malice. They are gossips, slanderers, God-haters, insolent, arrogant and boastful; they invent ways of doing evil; they disobey their parents; they have no understanding, no fidelity, no love, no mercy. Although they know God's righteous decree that those who do such things deserve death, they not only

continue to do these very things but also approve of those who practice them."

Apostle James also pulls no punches:

What causes fights and quarrels among you? Don't they come from your desires that battle within you? You desire but do not have, so you kill. You covet but you cannot get what you want, so you quarrel and fight. You do not have because you do not ask God. When you ask, you do not receive, because you ask with wrong motives, that you may spend what you get on your pleasures. (James 4:1–3 NIV)

We can add abuse and bullying of adults and even children! Whether it is physical, emotional, sexual, or mental abuse, it is all very damaging psychologically to the violated person. There is even abuse of animals as we see on the SPCA commercials. How sick is all of this. Yet there are people who would deny that sin is real.

Some people even go off the deep end in hating not only God but their fellow created beings so much that they kill in public places like our malls, schools, etc. Worse, tyrants such as Adolf Hitler, Joseph Stalin, Mao Tse-Tung, for example. murdered more than one hundred million people in wars and holocausts forcing their godless political ideologies upon humanity in the last century.

Humankind is guilty of monstrous atrocities against their own kind. Creatures in the animal kingdom may fight for dominance or to protect a territory or herd, but they do not kill their challenger. They just drive him off. The tragedy of the sinful human nature is that only humans destroy their own species. Power and control over fellow beings is more highly sought than the Lord's Golden Rule to love your neighbor as yourself. The power mongers even killed Jesus to maintain control over the people!

Summary

1. So, the first answer to the question of why there is evil is that God created free will so we could love. But we, humankind, chose instead of love, not to love and to disobey God. We chose to pursue power and our own self-centered passions, pleasures, desires, and wants, even when it comes at the expense of others, even their lives, and even if those actions are in direct disobedience to our Creator. So let us not blame shift the evil we create onto God. It is we who have brought evil into the world not God, and it is we who continually pursue it and encourage others to sin likewise!

2. Second, God allows (in His permissive will) evil to exist so love can exist. For love to exist, there must be free will, to choose not to love. God hopes we will rise above our selfishness and choose the more excellent way of love. The self-centered Gollum creature J. R. R. Tolkien portrayed in *Lord of the Rings* shows the fight between good and evil inside of us. God allows evil because He allows us. God could quickly eliminate the evil on the planet by eliminating us! He did it once by the Flood. Next time, we are warned, will be by fire—probably nuclear holocaust—and it is we, not God, who push the button.

3. There is evil because our priorities are self-centered not God centered. "But when the Pharisees heard that He had silenced the Sadducees, they gathered together. Then one of them, a lawyer, asked Him a question, testing Him, and saying, Teacher, which is the great commandment in the law? Jesus said to him, 'You shall love the LORD your God with all your heart, with all your soul, and with all your mind. This is the first and great commandment. And the second is like it: 'You shall love your neighbor as yourself.' On these two commandments hang all the Law and the Prophets.'" (Matthew 22:34–40 NKJV) So, our free will is to be used to love our Creator, our fellow man, and ourselves.

4. We need to pursue God's power of love instead of our love of power, which is the root cause of our evil freewill choices.

5

What Is God's Response to Our Freewill Choice of Disobedience to Him?

In Genesis 3:1–24 (NIV) we read:

Now the serpent was more crafty than any of the wild animals the LORD God had made. He said to the woman, "Did God really say, 'You must not eat from any tree in the garden?'"

The woman said to the serpent, "We may eat fruit from the trees in the garden, but God did say, 'You must not eat fruit from the tree that is in the middle of the garden, and you must not touch it, or you will die.'"

"You will not certainly die," the serpent said to the woman. "For God knows that when you eat from it your eyes will be opened, and you will be like God, knowing good and evil."

When the woman saw that the fruit of the tree was good for food and pleasing to the eye, and also desirable for gaining wisdom, she took some and ate it. She also gave some to her husband, who was with her, and he ate it. Then the eyes of both of them were opened, and they realized they were naked; so they sewed fig leaves together and made coverings for themselves.

Then the man and his wife heard the sound of the Lord God as he was walking in the garden in the cool of the day, and they hid from the Lord God among the trees of the garden. But the Lord God called to the man, "Where are you?"

He answered, "I heard you in the garden, and I was afraid because I was naked; so I hid."

And he said, "Who told you that you were naked? Have you eaten from the tree that I commanded you not to eat from?"

The man said, "The woman you put here with me— she gave me some fruit from the tree, and I ate it."

Then the Lord God said to the woman, "What is this you have done?"

The woman said, "The serpent deceived me, and I ate."

So the Lord God said to the serpent, "Because you have done this,

> *"Cursed are you above all livestock*
> *and all wild animals!*
> *You will crawl on your belly*
> *and you will eat dust*
> *all the days of your life.*
> *And I will put enmity*
> *between you and the woman,*

and between your offspring[a] and hers;
he will crush[b] your head,
and you will strike his heel."

To the woman he said,

"I will make your pains in childbearing very
severe;
with painful labor you will give birth to children.
Your desire will be for your husband,
and he will rule over you."

To Adam he said, "Because you listened to your wife
and ate fruit from the tree about which I commanded
you, 'You must not eat from it,'

"Cursed is the ground because of you;
through painful toil you will eat food from it
all the days of your life.
It will produce thorns and thistles for you,
and you will eat the plants of the field.
By the sweat of your brow
you will eat your food
until you return to the ground,
since from it you were taken;
for dust you are
and to dust you will return."

Adam[c] named his wife Eve,[d] because she would
become the mother of all the living.

The Lord God made garments of skin for Adam and
his wife and clothed them. And the Lord God said,
"The man has now become like one of us, knowing
good and evil. He must not be allowed to reach out

his hand and take also from the tree of life and eat, and live forever." So the LORD God banished him from the Garden of Eden to work the ground from which he had been taken. After he drove the man out, he placed on the east side[c] of the Garden of Eden cherubim and a flaming sword flashing back and forth to guard the way to the tree of life.

As verse 22 says, since we have become like God knowing good and evil, we were removed from the Garden so we could not eat of the tree of life and live forever in a state of disobedience. By being separated from the tree of life, we introduced death into the world.

The Lord takes our sinful conduct in our life very seriously and holds us accountable for what we do, how we respect Him, and how we treat others.

In Romans 1:18–25, 28, apostle Paul writes:

The wrath of God is being revealed from heaven against all the godlessness and wickedness of people, who suppress the truth by their wickedness, since what may be known about God is plain to them, because God has made it plain to them. For since the creation of the world God's invisible qualities—his eternal power and divine nature—have been clearly seen, being understood from what has been made, so that people are without excuse.

For although they knew God, they neither glorified him as God nor gave thanks to him, but their thinking became futile and their foolish hearts were darkened. Although they claimed to be wise, they became fools and exchanged the glory of the immortal God for images made to look like a mortal human being and birds and animals and reptiles.

Therefore God gave them over in the sinful desires of their hearts to sexual impurity for the degrading of their bodies with one another. They exchanged the truth about God for a lie, and worshiped and served created things rather than the Creator—who is forever praised. Amen.

Furthermore, just as they did not think it worthwhile to retain the knowledge of God, so God gave them over to a depraved mind, so that they do what ought not to be done. (NIV)

The last verse says we are turned over to a depraved mind. That means that God exacts a very severe punishment for our disobedience. He turns us over to ourselves!

Our disobedience to our Creator's wishes—our sin—has separated us from Him. After Adam ate the forbidden fruit of the knowledge of good and evil, God cries out: "Adam… where are you?" in Genesis 3:9 (NKJV). Of course, God knew He was behind palm tree number 666. (Just a wild guess at the number) God was asking something else. You have broken covenant with me, where are you going from here? Sin means to miss the mark. The mark is God's standard of righteousness and holiness.

If you were able to perfectly keep all 629 commandments in the Old Testament, called the law, during your whole life, then you would be considered righteous before God, the righteous judge.

But in Romans 3:10–20 (NIV) apostle Paul points out:

As it is written: "There is no one righteous, not even one;

there is no one who understands; there is no one who seeks God.

All have turned away; they have together become worthless; there is no one who does good, not even one."

"Their throats are open graves; their tongues practice deceit." The poison of vipers is on their lips."

"Their mouths are full of cursing and bitterness."

"Their feet are swift to shed blood;

ruin and misery mark their ways,

and the way of peace they do not know."

"There is no fear of God before their eyes."

Now we know that whatever the law says, it says to those who are under the law, so that every mouth may be silenced and the whole world held accountable to God.

Therefore no one will be declared righteous in God's sight by the works of the law; rather, through the law we become conscious of our sin.

Michelangelo artistically portrays this on the ceiling of the Sistine Chapel by showing man with a limp hand unable to save himself but an engaged God reaching out to His lost creation. We have done all the sinning; we cannot save ourselves. Our good deeds, the Apostle Paul says, are like filthy rags before a holy God. We have done all the sinning; God has done all the saving by providing another way of obtaining righteousness through Jesus's atoning death and resurrection.

Receiving Righteousness by Grace through Faith in Jesus Christ:

Since no one can perfectly keep the law, God provided another way of becoming righteous:

> But now apart from the law the righteousness of God has been made known, to which the Law and the Prophets testify. This righteousness is given through faith in[b] Jesus Christ to all who believe. There is no difference between Jew and Gentile, for all have sinned and fallen short of the glory of God, and all are justified freely by his grace through the redemption that came by Christ Jesus. God presented Christ as a sacrifice of atonement,[c] through the shedding of his blood—to be received by faith. He did this to demonstrate his righteousness, because in his forbearance he had left the sins committed beforehand unpunished—he did it to demonstrate his righteousness at the present time, so as to be just and the one who justifies those who have faith in Jesus. (Romans 3:21–26 NIV).

Captain John Newton was a slave ship captain who tore thousands of Africans from their homes to be slaves in America. Of course, the Arab merchants and African tribes who kidnapped these innocent people from their homes were complicit as well, in addition to the wealthy slave traders in America and England who sold the slaves to the plantation owners. On one passage, his ship ran into a major storm in the middle of the Atlantic. As the ship was breaking up and all souls were going to be lost, including his, he got on his knees and repented of his wicked ways. He committed the rest of his life to fighting the slave trade in England. It took William Wilberforce, a member of Parliament, and Newton twenty-five years to have Parliament stop the use of English ships transporting slaves! Why? Because it was too lucrative! Also, as a result of his conversion, John Newton wrote one of our greatest hymns, "Amazing Grace How Sweet the Sound that Saved a Wretch Like Me." Captain Newton said, "I am a great sinner, and Christ is a great savior." Apostle Paul states: "But thank God! He gives us victory over sin and death through our Lord Jesus Christ" (1 Corinthians 15:57 NLT).

> *But God demonstrates His own love toward us, in that while we were still sinners, Christ died for us. (Romans 5:8 NKJV)*

So, God's response to us bringing sin and death into the world is to provide another way of going to heaven since our good works are stained with sin. At the cross of Christ, He takes upon Himself the just punishment for our sins and offers us forgiveness of our sins if we turn away (repent) from our sins and surrender our will to following His will in our lives.

> *God showed how much he loved us by sending his one and only Son into the world so that we might have eternal life through him." (1 John 4:9 NLT)*

Will you ask God to forgive your sins by accepting Christ's death on the cross for your sins and start to follow Jesus today?

> *For God so loved the world that he gave his one and only Son, that whoever believes in him shall not perish but have eternal life. (John 3:16 NASB)*

6

What Is Love?

We saw in chapter 3 that our Creator wanted to create a being in His image that was both physical and spiritual, with self-awareness, with a totally independent volition, making its own uncontrolled decisions and choices, and most importantly having the capacity to love. To love God, to love others, and to love itself. You can program a computer to do those things, but it is only following its program; it is not doing these things on its own volition. Well fortunately, at least the AI is not there yet! There are many movies like *The Matrix* and *I Robot* where machines who can think for themselves end up ruling the world. That is for a distant time in the future; we hope never.

At this point, it is important to define what love is so we can see why God thought it was so important. At the present time in Western civilization, we have just one word for love. We must identify its meaning from the context in which we use it. For example, saying "I love ice cream" and "I love you" to a spouse mean different things using the same word. Other cultures are more precise than we are. They have different words for love based on the context.

So, for help defining the term, we will turn to classical Greece, with all those clever philosophers with nothing better to do than lounge around in tunics enjoying those drop-dead gorgeous views of the Aegean. They invested a lot of time figuring many things out for us.

Today we use the word love in many ways. For example, "I love that car," "I love to watch baseball," "I love my spouse," etc. Each of these has a different meaning depending upon the context. In contrast, the ancient Greek culture had multiple words for love because each one expresses a different form of emotional attachment to other people and things. In *The Four Loves*, C. S. Lewis describes the four main kinds of love. In a recent book _How Should We Live? Great Ideas from the Past for Everyday Life_, by Roman Krznaric, six kinds of love are cited. Indeed, who does not want to learn from the past! Why make the mistakes and missed opportunities others have? Both C. S. Lewis's, and Mr. Krznaric's descriptions are highly informative, so we will use them here. Together, they have identified seven kinds of love. I have added a few comments from my own reservoir of ignorance on the whole subject! But what more can you expect from a dull and boring engineer!

1. Eros; Romantic and Sexual Passion

Mr. Krznaric writes: "_eros_ was named after the Greek god of fertility, and it represented the idea of sexual passion and desire. But the Greeks didn't always think of it as something positive, as we tend to do today. In fact, _eros_ was viewed as a dangerous, fiery, and irrational form of love that could take hold of you and possess you—an attitude shared by later spiritual thinkers, such as the Christian writer C. S. Lewis."

"_Eros_ involved a loss of control that frightened the Greeks. Which is odd, because losing control is precisely what many people seek in a relationship. Don't we all hope to fall 'madly' or hopelessly in love?" Losing all our good sense in the process!

2. Philia; deep friendship like a brother or sister

Mr. Krznaric writes: "Brotherly love was philia or friendship, which the Greeks valued far more than the base sexuality of eros. Philia concerned the deep comradely friendship that developed between brothers in arms who had fought side by side on the battlefield. It was about showing loyalty to your friends, sacrificing for them, as well as sharing your emotions with them. (Another kind of philia, sometimes called **Storge**, embodied the love between parents and their children.)"

But to have a deep friendship, we first must be a friend. This is an earned relationship through investing time, sharing similar interests, even similar beliefs. The mere collection of "friends" on social media is not the strong bonding of brotherly love.

We get the word Philadelphia, meaning City of Brotherly Love, from *Philia*; love and Adelphia from the Greek for "brotherhood," *αδέλφια*, or from the same womb.

3. Ludus, or playful love

Mr. Krznaric writes: "While philia could be a matter of great seriousness, there was a third type of love valued by the ancient Greeks, which was playful love. Following the Roman poet Ovid, scholars (such as the philosopher A. C. Grayling) commonly use the Latin word *ludus* to describe this form of love, which concerns the playful affection between children or casual lovers. We've all had a taste of it in the flirting and teasing in the early stages of a relationship. But we also live out our ludus when we sit around in a bar bantering and laughing with friends, or when we go out dancing."

4. Pragma, or long-standing love

Mr. Krznaric writes: "The use of the ancient Greek root *pragma* as a form of love was popularized by the Canadian sociologist John Allen Lee in the 1970s, who described it as a mature, realistic love that is commonly found amongst long-established couples. Pragma is about making compromises to help the relationship work over time and showing patience and tolerance. There is in fact little evidence that the Greeks commonly used this precise term themselves, so it is best thought of as a modern update on the ancient Greek loves.

"The psychoanalyst Erich Fromm said that we expend too much energy on "falling in love" and need to learn more how to "stand in love." Pragma is precisely about standing in love—trying to give love rather than just receive it. With about a third of first marriages in the U.S. ending through divorce or separation in the first 10 years, we should surely think about bringing a serious dose of *pragma* into our relationships."

Not to mention an overall 50 percent divorce rate in the West! But who's counting? Half of my guy friends are jealous I am single, and I am jealous that they are at least married, even if it has been several times. After all, nobody's perfect, which is, of course, precisely the point of Pragma love. The stick it out anyway love. A wise man once told me, when you are young you marry because you "fall in love." But since it is highly emotionally based, you can just as quickly fall out of love when finances change, your spouse is in a disfiguring accident, etc., etc. When you are older, he said, you marry for convenience. Convenience may not be the highest form of love, but it at least is based on a long-term commitment to working things out, instead of abandoning ship when problems start arising, and in any relationship, they will arise. My sister adds that since everyone has problems, you pick someone to marry whose set of problems you can live with!

Sorry for being so pragmatic about this, but after all the word for this love is *pragma*!

5. Philautia, Self-Love

Mr. Krznaric writes: "The Greeks fifth variety of love was philautia or self-love. And clever Greeks such as Aristotle realized there were two types. One was an unhealthy variety associated with narcissism, where you became self-obsessed and focused on personal fame and fortune. Some writers would associate this kind of love with the 'Ego'. A me first, self centered love. A healthier version enhanced your wider capacity to love. Like having a healthy self respect.

"The idea was that if you like yourself and feel secure in yourself, you will have plenty of love to give others. Or, as Aristotle put it, 'All friendly feelings for others are an extension of a man's feelings for himself.'

"The ancient Greeks found diverse kinds of love in relationships with a wide range of people—friends, family, spouses, strangers, and even themselves. This contrasts with our typical focus on a single romantic relationship, where we hope to find all the different loves wrapped into a single person or soul mate. The message from the Greeks is to nurture the varieties of love and tap into its many sources. Don't just seek eros, but cultivate philia by spending more time with old friends, or develop ludus by dancing the night away.

"Moreover, we should abandon our obsession with perfection. Don't expect your partner to offer you all the varieties of love, all of the time (with the danger that you may toss aside a partner who fails to live up to your desires). Recognize that a relationship may begin with plenty of eros and ludus, then evolve toward embodying more pragma or agape."

We will address the dangers of the ego; self-love in another chapter. Suffice to say that history teaches us that the bad kind of self-love, the ego, is self-destructive to individuals, and to an entire nation when ruled by a megalomaniac (a person with delusions of self-importance and needing admiration), a narcissist (self-importance with lack of empathy for others), egocentric (self-centered), ruler as all tyrants are.

6. Affection Love

In C. S. Lewis's *The Four Loves*, he describes a love called "affection love." This is an affection for things. For example, "I love ice cream," "I love baseball."

On the other hand, "I love our dog, Sammy," for example, Mr. Krznaric would put with Philia or Ludus type of love, since most family pets are treated with more love than just mere affection. They are considered a family member, which is why we cry at their passing. We do not cry when the ice cream melts. Our pets are truly loved, and they return that love. Therefore, we are so appalled by animal cruelty. It is unfathomable that a human soul would be so callous as to hurt our family friends. But perhaps those individuals were never loved. Jesus said to love one another even as I have loved you; in the parable of the Good Samaritan, He shows us to love even our enemies, which leads us to agape love.

7. Agape Selfless Love

Both Messieurs Krznaric and Lewis describe this kind of love as the highest form of love. It is opposite to self-love. It requires that "self" step aside so self-sacrificial love can move in. Agape is selfless love. When the New Testament was written, this kind of love was given the name agape for the first time, though it had always existed. It describes self-sacrificial love. This was a love that you extended to all people, whether family members or distant strangers, even enemies. Agape was later translated into Latin as *caritas*, which is the origin of our word *charity*.

This is the type of love that a parent has for his or her child; indeed, a mother will even die defending her child. Mother Theresa had this love for the least among us. Her selfless love for the poorest of the poor was so well respected that presidents, prime ministers, and princesses like Lady Diana visited her. Indeed, she was so respected that one million Hindus attended her Catholic funeral!

Agape culminates in Jesus, whose self-sacrificial love for us on the cross at Calvary brings the hope of redemption to a sinful humankind:

> *But God demonstrates His own love (agape) toward us, in that while we were yet sinners, Christ died for us. (Romans 5:8 NASB)*

> *For God so loved (agape) the world, that He gave His only begotten Son, that whoever believes in Him shall not perish, but have eternal life. (John 3:16 NASB)*

C. S. Lewis referred to agape as "gift love," the highest form of Christian love.

For a more detailed discussion of the seven loves, including a full list of scholarly references, please see Roman Krznaric's book *How Should We Live? Great Ideas from the Past for Everyday Life*. Also, see C. S. Lewis's *The Four Loves*.

7

Love our Enemies?

That Jesus would teach us the counterintuitive concept to love even our enemies shows that Love is a choice, not a feeling. After all, no one feels like loving his enemy.

Jesus challenges us:

> *If you love those who love you, what credit is that to you? Even sinners love those who love them. And if you do good to those who are good to you, what credit is that to you? Even sinners do that. And if you lend to those from whom you expect repayment, what credit is that to you? Even sinners lend to sinners, expecting to be repaid in full. But love your enemies, do good to them, and lend to them without expecting to get anything back. Then your reward will be great, and you will be children of the Most High, because he is kind to the ungrateful and wicked. Be merciful, just as your Father is merciful." (Luke 6:32–36 NIV)*

Jesus also spoke of loving one's neighbor, but He defines neighbor not as the person living next to you, but the person who is the most different from you, the kind of person you least respect, least want to be around. Jesus's famous parable of the Good Samaritan found in Luke 10 occurred at a time Samaritans and Jews had little respect for each other.

In Luke 10, in reply to the question of who my neighbor is,

> *Jesus said: "A man was going down from Jerusalem to Jericho, when he was attacked by robbers. They stripped him of his clothes, beat him and went away,*

leaving him half dead. A priest happened to be going down the same road, and when he saw the man, he passed by on the other side. So too, a Levite, when he came to the place and saw him, passed by on the other side. But a Samaritan, as he traveled, came where the man was; and when he saw him, he took pity on him. He went to him and bandaged his wounds, pouring on oil and wine. Then he put the man on his own donkey, brought him to an inn and took care of him. The next day he took out two denarii[c] and gave them to the innkeeper. 'Look after him,' he said, 'and when I return, I will reimburse you for any extra expense you may have.' Which of these three do you think was a neighbor to the man who fell into the hands of robbers?" The expert in the law replied, "The one who had mercy on him." (Luke 10:30–37 NIV)

Jesus told him and now tells us, "Go and do likewise."

8

Risking Love

We only have to watch the news to see that there is growing evidence that agape is in a dangerous decline in many countries. Empathy levels in the United States have declined sharply over the past forty years, with the steepest fall occurring in the past decade. We urgently need to revive our capacity to care about strangers.

The diverse Greek system of loves applied in our lives can provide personal wholeness. Mr. Krznaric writes: "By mapping out the extent to which all six loves are present in your life, you might discover you've got a lot more love than you had ever imagined—even if you feel an absence of a physical lover."

"It's time we introduced the six varieties of Greek love into our everyday way of speaking and thinking. If the art of coffee deserves its own sophisticated vocabulary, then why not the art of love?"

In *The Four Loves*, C. S. Lewis writes:

> *To love at all is to be vulnerable. Love anything and your heart will be wrung and possibly broken. If you want to make sure of keeping it intact you must give it to no one, not even an animal. Wrap it carefully round with hobbies and little luxuries; avoid all entanglements. Lock it up safe in the casket or coffin of your selfishness. But in that casket, safe, dark, motionless, airless, it will change. It will not be broken; it will become unbreakable, impenetrable, irredeemable. Therefore, to love is to be vulnerable.*

But who wants an impenetrable, irredeemable heart? That cost is even higher than having a broken heart. A broken heart the Lord can heal. Psalm 147:3 (NASB) says: "He heals the brokenhearted and binds up their wounds." So, take a chance in life to risk your love's rejection whether it is in relationships or serving others; it will someday pay off, and in the meantime, the rejection can be healed over time.

Will you use your free will to risk loving God and others today?

9

How to Love

Now that we know what kinds of love there are, and that we need to love even our enemies and we need to risk loving, even if it is spurned, rejected, or ridiculed, no discussion of the subject would be complete without informing us how to love. For this, we turn to one of the most learned rabbis of his day, the Apostle Paul. In 1 Corinthians 13 (NIV) he writes:

> [1]*If I speak in the tongues* [a] *of men or of angels, but do not have love, I am only a resounding gong or a clanging cymbal.* [2]*If I have the gift of prophecy and can fathom all mysteries and all knowledge, and if I have a faith that can move mountains, but do not have love, I am nothing.* [3]*If I give all I possess to the poor and give over my body to hardship that I may boast,* [b] *but do not have love, I gain nothing.*
>
> [4]*Love is patient, love is kind. It does not envy, it does not boast, it is not proud.* [5]*It does not dishonor others, it is not self-seeking, it is not easily angered, it keeps no record of wrongs.* [6]*Love does not delight in evil but rejoices with the truth.* [7]*It always protects, always trusts, always hopes, always perseveres.*
>
> [8]*Love never fails. But where there are prophecies, they will cease; where there are tongues, they will be stilled; where there is knowledge, it will pass away.* [9]*For we know in part and we prophesy in part,* [10]*but when completeness comes, what is in part disappears.*

11When I was a child, I talked like a child, I thought like a child, I reasoned like a child. When I became a man, I put the ways of childhood behind me. 12For now we see only a reflection as in a mirror; then we shall see face to face. Now I know in part; then I shall know fully, even as I am fully known.

13And now these three remain: faith, hope and love. But the greatest of these is love. (1 Corinthians 13:1–13)

10

Can God Make a Rock He Cannot Pick Up?

Discrediting God by Putting Him in No-Win Situations

There is an age-old quandary questioning God's omnipotence—His all-powerfulness. The question asks: Can God make a rock so large that He cannot pick it up? This question is to set up a Catch-22 situation. For if God cannot make such a rock, then He is not all powerful. But if He can make such a rock, then He is still not all-powerful because He cannot pick it up! The question is posed so either way God loses. Sometimes these questions are asked as a purely innocent intellectual pursuit. But sometimes questions that attempt to put God down are asked to discredit God or His attributes or are even attempts to show it is foolish to believe in Him. Indeed, if we can dismiss the thought of an all-powerful God, then we have less to fear in rebelling against Him. We can become our own masters of the universe; we can become the gods of our world. If God is not all-powerful, then we may even be able to usurp the role of God for ourselves! If we can be in charge of the universe or even our own little universe here on earth, then we do not have to listen to or submit to the rules, laws, decrees, teachings, etc. of the Lord of the universe. We can be a law unto ourselves and do whatever we want with no limitations!

On more than one occasion, there were those who wanted to discredit Jesus, as He was becoming extremely popular among the people. Thousands were following His teachings. This threatened the status quo, so some of the religious leaders tried to discredit Him by putting Him into no-win situations, as we find for example in John 8 (NKJV):

Now early in the morning He came again into the temple, and all the people came to Him; and He sat down and taught them. Then the scribes and Pharisees brought to Him a woman caught in adultery. And when they had set her in the midst, they said to Him, "Teacher, this woman was caught in adultery, in the very act. Now Moses, in the law, commanded us that such should be stoned. But what do You say?" This they said, testing Him, that they might have something of which to accuse Him. But Jesus stooped down and wrote on the ground with His finger, as though He did not hear.

So when they continued asking Him, He raised Himself up and said to them, "He who is without sin among you, let him throw a stone at her first. And again He stooped down and wrote on the ground. Then those who heard it, being convicted by their conscience, went out one by one, beginning with the oldest even to the last. And Jesus was left alone, and the woman standing in the midst. When Jesus had raised Himself up and saw only the woman, He said to her, "Woman, where are those accusers of yours? Has no one condemned you?"

She said, "No one, Lord."

And Jesus said to her, "Neither do I condemn you; go and sin no more."

Then Jesus spoke to them again, saying, "I am the light of the world. He who follows Me shall not walk in darkness, but have the light of life." (John 8:2–12)

Here, the religious leaders tried to put Jesus in a no-win situation, like God making the rock scenario. If Jesus doesn't approve stoning the woman caught in adultery, He breaks the Jewish law found in Deuteronomy 22:22–24, consequently no one can continue to follow Him. If He approves it, He breaks the Roman law that prohibits Jews from carrying out capital punishment. (That is why later the Jewish leaders must go to the governor, Pontius Pilate, to get permission to get the Romans to kill Jesus). They have set the trap, putting Jesus in a lose-lose situation. They have Him where they can finally discredit Him. It's over for Jesus.

In response, Jesus turns the tables on them. He turns the issue from her sin to their sins! He says to them, let him who is without sin cast the first stone! Then, amazingly, the passage says, from the eldest to the youngest, they drop their stones and leave because their hearts are convicted that their lives are no purer than hers. Had they thrown a stone, they would have been condemning themselves along with her. In the Lord's presence, they and us are convicted of our own sins. It is of interest to note that the man was not caught along with the woman, probably because it was a male-dominated good old boys culture. Indeed, the only sinless one there who could have thrown a stone was Jesus Himself! They drop their stones and leave. Then Jesus shows He has the authority to forgive sins, which only God can do. Remember that at His birth, He is pronounced Emmanuel, "God with Us." So, He chooses to forgive her: "Woman neither do I condemn you, go and sin no more." This is a foreshadowing of His purpose for coming to earth—to forgive our sins at His death on the cross of Calvary.

We should also keep in mind that not all the religious leaders were against Jesus; Nicodemus and others eventually follow Him.

Now back to our seemingly impossible trap that insinuates that either way God is not all-powerful. If He makes a rock he cannot pick up or cannot make a rock He can't pick up, either way He is not all-powerful. Either way, God loses. He cannot be omnipotent, the philosophers conclude.

God's Nature

Just as the people holding the stones clearly did not understand the nature of God's justice and mercy until confronted directly by Him in the person of Jesus—Emmanuel—it is the same with this rock quandary. We need to understand God's nature to understand Him. That is a lifelong study. We have the benefit of two thousand years of learning about God by Him reveling Himself to us from Job to Jesus. In this case, yes, God is all-powerful—omnipotent. But His all-powerfulness is transcended by His will. His strength is controlled by His will. So, if God chooses not to be able to pick up the rock, then He cannot, and a moment later if He chooses to pick it up, He can. God's omnipotence is controlled by His will. In the next chapter we will see what characteristic of God controls His will!

11

Is There Anything the Omnipotent God Can't Do?

If God is God, He should be able to do anything, right? Then can He do evil? We saw in the last chapter that God's power is controlled by His will. God's will is controlled by another essential character trait, His holiness. The choices He makes are transcended, governed, controlled, and constrained by His holiness. God is so purely good, so righteous, so completely holy and just that He cannot even look upon evil, let alone think evil thoughts or do evil deeds!

Habakkuk 1:13 (New American Standard Bible 1995) reveals to us:

> *Your eyes are too pure to approve evil, And You can not look on wickedness with favor.*

Pastor Steve Shirley notes that the Hebrew word for "look on" is *nabat*. *Strong's Concordance* gives this definition: "look intently at; by implication to regard with pleasure, favor, or care." So, the NASB correctly amends the word *favorably* to the verse. So, what can't God do? He cannot do evil, nor look upon it with favor. His will, choices, and actions are constrained by his holiness.

12

Would God Command You to Do Evil?

When my college philosophy professor found out I was a believing Christian, he asked me if God commanded me to pick up a child and dash its brains against a brick wall would I do it?

My initial answer surprised him. I asked if I could have some time on that! He smiled, and probably thought, *What kind of person can't say an immediate no!* Then he said take all the time I needed. Well of course he knew, and we all know, that such a heinous act is terribly wrong. Though even today all around the world we see religious zealots murdering men, women, and even children in the name of their god.

I heard the question differently. I heard, *Would the God of the Bible ask me or tell me to do such a thing?* Of course, the professor was too moral and wouldn't ask such a terrible thing, but maybe God could, and then what would I do? So, I needed time to search out whether the Lord would ask such a question. As Christians, what kind of God do we serve?

It did not take long. Soon after during a daily devotional time, I was lead to Jeremiah 32:32–35 (NIV):

> *The people of Israel and Judah have provoked me by all the evil they have done—they, their kings and officials, their priests and prophets, the people of Judah and those living in Jerusalem. They turned their backs to me and not their faces; though I taught them again and again, they would not listen or respond to discipline. They set up their vile images in the house that bears my Name and defiled it. They built high places for Baal*

in the Valley of Ben Hinnom to sacrifice their sons
and daughters to Molek, though I never commanded—
nor did it enter my mind—that they should do such a
detestable thing and so make Judah sin.

Wow! The omniscient God who knows all things and thinks all things not only would not command killing children, which answered the professor's question, but even the thought of doing such a heinous act *never even crossed His mind!* God is so holy, so pure, that even His thoughts are constrained by His holiness! There are things you and I will think and talk about that would never even cross God's mind! The fact that the professor and I would entertain such a discussion shows how sinful we were. The professor and I thought we were righteous for not being willing to kill the child, but God is so holy that even the thought of it never even crossed His mind, and He has never commanded such a thing!

The professor was speechless, as all of us sinners are when confronted with the pure holiness of the God of the Bible.

In 1 Peter 1:15–17 (NASB) we are exhorted:

> *But [a]like the Holy One who called you, [b]be holy*
> *yourselves also in all your behavior; because it is*
> *written: "YOU SHALL BE HOLY, FOR I AM HOLY."*
>
> *If you address as Father the One who impartially*
> *judges according to each one's work, conduct*
> *yourselves in fear during the time of your stay on*
> *earth.*

13

Why Does God Seem to Hide?

Many of us, especially in times of trouble, ask where God is in all of this. Even during normal circumstances, He seems to hide. Some 90 percent of Americans believe God exists. We believe He is out there, somewhere, but He doesn't seem to be very involved in this world. Or is He? We may even feel He is not involved in our lives. It is true you can live your whole life absent of any personal connection with God. Some people do this intentionally because they are angry at Him for something bad that occurred in their lives, like the loss of a loved one, loss of a job, or a relationship, etc. I know a man who lost his family in the Holocaust and was so angry at God for allowing it that he turned his back on God for his whole life. Some people choose to ignore Him so they can be their own boss, not wanting God, Jesus, or the Bible telling them what to do. Other people just don't know God wants to be involved in their lives.

Where is God? There is no phone number or website to contact Him. We cannot look up and see Him sitting on some heavenly throne. So, does God hide? Well, He does, and He doesn't. If we want to come to know God, we must come on His terms not ours. The next chapter shows you how.

14

Is there a Way to See God?

There are many verses in the Bible that show us what we must do to "see" our heavenly father.

"For the eyes of the LORD range throughout the earth to strengthen those whose hearts are fully committed to him" (2 Chronicles 16:9 NIV). So, the first thing we learn is that God is actively searching out for those who are "fully committed to him."

"But if from there you seek the Lord your God, you will find him if you seek him with all your heart and with all your soul" (Deuteronomy 4:29 NIV). God isn't hiding from us. He's right now in our presence and desiring a close relationship with us. If we "seek" (look for) Him, we will find Him.

First Timothy 2:3–4 (NASB 1995) says, "This is good and acceptable in the sight of God our Savior, who desires all men to be saved and to come to the knowledge of the truth." The Lord wants us to come to Him!

"And without faith it is impossible to please God, because anyone who comes to him must believe that he exists and that he rewards those who earnestly seek him" (Hebrews 11:6 NLT). Obviously, our seeking will involve faith—believing that He is there. Then, He rewards us by revealing Himself to us.

In Psalm 63 (KJV), King David, who is being hunted down by his son, Absalom, who has seized control of the throne, is hiding out in the desert of Judea. David laments his fate, but this bad predicament has brought him around to seeking for something even larger than his problem—a relationship with his Creator. And that should be our response to the overwhelming problems in our lives. Hear what David said in Psalm 63:1–8:

*O God, thou art my God; earnestly will I seek thee:
My soul thirsteth for thee, my flesh longeth for thee,
in a dry and weary land, where no water is.*

*So have I looked upon thee in the sanctuary, to see
thy power and thy glory.*

*Because thy loving kindness is better than life, My
lips shall praise thee.*

*So will I bless thee while I live: I will lift up my hands
in thy name.*

*My soul shall be satisfied as with marrow and fatness;
And my mouth shall praise thee with joyful lips;*

*When I remember thee upon my bed, And meditate
on thee in the night-watches.*

*For thou hast been my help, And in the shadow of
thy wings will I rejoice.*

*My soul followeth hard after thee: Thy right hand
upholdeth me.*

This psalm is immensely powerful. The human soul of David the psalmist "thirsts" and "follows hard" for its creator, like a man out in the desert is solely focused on finding water!

King David said: "As the deer longs for streams of water, so I long for you, O God" (Psalm 42:1 NLT).

To seek God means to pursue Him alone to fill the God-shaped hole in your life, to have an intimate personal relationship with Him:

*But the hour is coming, and now is, when the true
worshipers will worship the Father in spirit and*

truth; for the Father is seeking such to worship Him. (John 4:23 NKJV)

God is waiting on us to seek after Him daily in prayer and Bible meditations. Through the presence of the Holy Spirit, we can be comforted and assured of His presence in our lives.

Therefore if you have been raised up with Christ, keep seeking the things above, where Christ is, seated at the right hand of God. [a]Set your mind on the things above, not on the things that are on earth. (Colossians 3:1–2 NASB)

This chapter encourages us to pursue Christ, not carnality.

The Greek verb translated "earnestly seeking" is in a form that implies intensity and concentrated effort. This involves one's whole being as Deuteronomy 6:4–5 (NIV) says:

Hear, O Israel: The LORD our God, the LORD is one. Love the LORD your God with all your heart and with all your soul and with all your strength.

If we are earnestly seeking the Lord, it is not some indifferent, self-sparing, halfhearted effort. Rather, we show genuine zeal in pursuing Him. Whether Jews or Gentiles, God encourages all people everywhere to seek Him (Acts 15:17).

This concept of earnestly pursuing, seeking, longing for something or someone should not be new to us. David was thirsty out in the desert, but his soul was even more thirsty for being close to God. If we want the promotion at work, we will be committed to the company and diligently pursue the company's best interest. If we want to grow our business, we will diligently and wholeheartedly pursue making that next sale. If we desire a relationship with a special person, we will diligently and earnestly pursue him or her. So, whether it is business or personal, if we want a desired outcome, we must pursue it. We cannot just sit back and expect business or a relationship to come to us. Who do we think we are, some king where others including God have to dote on us! God, like a business or another person, wants to see if we are serious about being involved with them by seeing if we will pursue and earnestly seek them or Him.

Are you wholeheartedly seeking Him, or are you seeking the things of this World? Jesus says a man cannot serve two masters.

Anthropomorphisms note:

Notice the use of words like *eyes of the Lord* or *heart of God* in these Bible passages; these are called anthropomorphisms, which is the attribution of human traits, emotions, or intentions to nonhuman entities. God is a Spirit being; He does not have a physical form having eyes or a heart, unless He assumes a human form, as in the case of Jesus, who the Bible calls Emmanuel—God with us. These words, like the heart of God, the right hand of God, etc. are ascribed to God to help us to understand the infinite in our limited finite frame of reference.

15

What Is the Age of Accountability, and Why Is It So Important?

Before we discuss the next difficult question, we need to understand an important church teaching.

Roman Catholics and many Protestant denominations believe in an age of accountability. Somewhere in adolescence between twelve to fourteen years of age young people become aware of their freedom of choice, their free will. If they die before this time, they go to heaven. If they die afterward, they are judged by their actions, as adults are. In Judaism, for example, a boy becomes a man at the age of thirteen. Children have been learning right from wrong all during their formative years, but most decisions are made for them. In adolescent years, they are beginning to make personal choices and decisions that affect their lives. They start to act as free moral agents. Previously they decided on who their friends would be, but now they are deciding whether to engage in various moral behaviors that they were not aware of as children. Do they treat others with respect no matter who they are, or do they become members of an exclusive clique at school that excludes more peers than it includes? Do they start engaging in social pathologies such as smoking, smoking pot—the gateway drug, start drinking, becoming aloof and disobedient to parents; or start to steal to get things, etc.?

I was informed by a middle school teacher that about 20 percent of fourteen-year-olds engage in sex and pot. In other words, teens start engaging in bad choices. Dr Phil McGraw's show portrays many of these young people who go down the wrong path. He is smart enough not to make excuses for them but to have them learn they are accountable for their decisions and for them to learn the consequences of their actions on themselves, their parents, and those around them. It is hard for young people today to make right choices when our society bombards them with so many bad choices, like the need to be sexy, thin, popular, pleasure seekers, fame seekers, accumulating possessions, etc. Parents, on the other hand, want their young people to pursue education, sports, and group activities like scouting, after-school clubs, etc., so there is a tension in many families. Again, just watch Dr. Phil's program to see the sad consequences of poor choices teenage young people make.

Children, those under the age of say twelve, are very different. They are just forming their ideas of self, God, nature, and of right and wrong. Children are highly impressionable, and, unfortunately, parents, teachers, and community group leaders around them can twist and corrupt their development and their value systems.

The basis for the belief that children who die go to heaven is found in Mark 10:13–16 (NIV):

> [13]*Now people were bringing the little children to Jesus for Him to place His hands on them, and the disciples rebuked those who brought them.*
>
> [14]*But when Jesus saw this, He was indignant and told them, "Let the little children come to Me, and do not hinder them! For the kingdom of God belongs to such as these.* [15]*Truly I tell you, anyone who does not receive the kingdom of God like a little child will never enter it."* [16]*And He took the children in His arms, placed His hands on them, and blessed them.*

See also Luke 18:15 and Matthew 18.

This verse about children "belonging" to God's kingdom has comforted untold thousands of parents and families who have lost a child to illness, cancer, accidents, conflicts, childbirth, etc. When children die, they go instantly into the arms of Jesus, dwelling in God's kingdom for eternity. In the twinkling of an eye, they pass from death into abundant life forever! Unfortunately, this is not so with adults, who God holds accountable for their sins.

16

Why Did the Children of Sodom and Gomorrah Die with Their Parents?

Part 1: The Corruption of Children

As discussed in the chapter on the age of accountability, children are highly impressionable. They watch and emulate the behaviors of those around them. In particular, their parents have a great influence over their lives. The Bible says the laws of God are written on our hearts. So, what happens when parents, teachers, society, et.al, corrupt the moral compass of a child? Here are some real-life examples of the personal and national tragedies that follow:

- I worked with an engineer from Germany who denied the Holocaust, the state-sponsored genocide of Jews by Nazi Germany, even fourty years after World War II! Why, because he was between five to nine years old during World War II, he was in the Hitler Youth League. It is like our Boy Scouts developing survival skills, and comradery, but that is where the similarity ends. In the Hitler Youth you were also indoctrinated into Nazism—national socialism— and their rightness of the crushing by force any ideology different from theirs. Just as the children of Sodom were taught by their parents and culture. We are starting to see this intolerance for the beliefs of others on our college campuses. For example, if you don't subscribe to the liberal party line on global warming, they try to shut down your speech, burn your books, and physically threaten you, just as the Nazi Brown Shirts did in the 1930s, burning books and beating opponents physically. So, the Hitler Youth grew up to become the Brown Shirts, and later the SS, enforcing Nazism onto German society and the world around them. Rev. Dietrich Bonheoffer, an evangelical Lutheran minister, spoke out against the evils of Nazism. He was hung on a meat hook till dead, not to mention six million Jews who the Hitler Youth children were taught were enemies of the state. These atrocities were committed without question, because they had been trained from youth to obey not God but the state. Even older German people, when they heard about the death camps, were appalled because they had been brought up in the Judeo-Christian values of the Lutheran Church. Not so the children under Hitler's reign who were trained to obey without questioning the national socialist state and the Nazi leaders. The salute Heil Hitler was the Nazi's pledge of allegiance to Hitler and his government. Those who disagreed were crushed.

- This indoctrination of children to unquestionably obey their leaders and destroy their opponents, including family members and friends, is the same in all totalitarian regimes.

- Communism also teaches in elementary schools the ideology that you may do whatever you want to shut down any opposing viewpoints. There is no tolerance for criticism of Communism and its leaders or of someone holding an opposing viewpoint. It is estimated that in China after World War II Mao Tse-Tung murdered one hundred million people to consolidate his power, Joseph Stalin murdered twenty million in Russia before the war to consolidate his power. In communist countries you are taught the state is more important than the person, and the state knows better how to run your life than you do. So, you are assigned what your job will be, where you will live, and what you are allowed to believe and not believe. For seventy years after the 1917 Communist Revolution in Russia, the Soviet Union banned the Bible; after all, it teaches the sanctity of human life, individual freedom, and the political liberty of the individual.

In the 1980s when US President Ronald Reagan bankrupted the Soviets in an arms race and challenged President Mikhail Gorbachev to "tear down this (Berlin) wall," Russia opened back up to the West and allowed the Bible back in. To mock the existence of God, Soviet teachers would put two plants in a classroom, one the government watered, and the other for God to water. When God's plant died, they said to the children, see, God does not exist, or He doesn't care like we do for the helpless plant, brainwashing the children early. Fortunately, not everyone in the Soviet Union was invited into the Communist Party, and the Soviets left the Russian Orthodox Church alone, thinking it would die out with the elderly. They did not want a counterrevolution. Hitler did the same, letting the Lutheran and Catholic churches alone. He would crush them later after he dominated the world.

- In North Korea even today teachers tell students that they need to tell them if their parents at home are speaking against the state and the glorious leader.
- NAMBLA, the North America Man Boy Love Association, teaches boys that it is okay to have sex with men.
- Islamic terrorists' camps teach children to cut off the heads of dolls they are told are infidels. This way it comes easy for them when they grow up.
- In some countries, Islamic schools teach the children to hate the great Satan—the USA—and the little Satan—Israel. Is it any wonder that eleven of the thirteen terrorists in 9/11 were from Saudi Arabia where they had been taught that hatred as children?
- Prior to World War II, while our Boy Scouts were learning how to tie knots and quote the Pledge of Allegiance about liberty and justice for all, in Japan, their children were being taught the Samurai warrior culture and total obedience to the emperor. In Germany, the Hitler Youth were taught the arts of war, racial superiority, and total obedience to the Fuehrer without question. The children were taught to crush any dissenting views. To even turn in their parents for criticizing the government!
- Today, in some countries, mere children are forced into sex trafficking. This dulls the moral consciences of the children. They are forced by using threats of pain, and by being kept drugged up.

- Today there are too many cases of sexual abuse inside families, which psychologically, physically, emotionally, and sexually damage the children.

What was the consequence of a generation of children in Nazi Germany, Imperial Japan, and Communist Russia being indoctrinated by their parents, schools, and governments into growing up believing they had a right to inflict their will and their godless ideology upon their neighbors, using their free will to ignore God and His love. The result was the world suffered the loss of sixty-eight million people, because too many of the sons and daughters of Germany, Japan, and Russia grew up believing they could force their will and ideology onto their neighbors. And for fifty years after World War II, hundreds of millions more were murdered and enslaved under communism.

Like the children cited above, the children of Sodom and Gomorrah were brought up by their parents and society to live a morally decadent lifestyle and to be disobedient to God and His laws. So, God took them into the safety of His kingdom, whereas we saw in the chapter on age of accountability in Mark 10:14–16 that they would sit with Jesus every day learning how to live and love rightly.

What does Jesus say about adults who corrupt their own and other children around them?

Jesus said to His disciples: "Things that cause people to stumble are bound to come, but woe to anyone through whom they come. It would be better for them to be thrown into the sea with a millstone tied around their neck than to cause one of these little ones to stumble. So watch yourselves (Luke 17:1–3 NIV).

What we teach the children today will affect the kind of world we will live in tomorrow.

17

What Were the Sins of Sodom and the Neighboring Cities that God Destroyed Them?

Part 2

First, in Genesis 18:16–33 (NIV), the Lord tells Abraham why he has come down to Sodom.

> *When the men (angels) got up to leave, they looked down toward Sodom, and Abraham walked along with them to see them on their way.*
>
> *Then the LORD said, "Shall I hide from Abraham what I am about to do?*
>
> *Abraham will surely become a great and powerful nation, and all nations on earth will be blessed through him.*
>
> *For I have chosen him, so that he will direct his children and his household after him to keep the way of the LORD by doing what is right and just, so that the LORD will bring about for Abraham what he has promised him."*
>
> *Then the LORD said, "The outcry against Sodom and Gomorrah is so great and their sin so grievous*

that I will go down and see if what they have done is as bad as the outcry that has reached me. If not, I will know."

The men turned away and went toward Sodom, but Abraham remained standing before the LORD.

Then Abraham approached him and said: "Will you sweep away the righteous with the wicked?

What if there are fifty righteous people in the city? Will you really sweep it away and not spare the place for the sake of the fifty righteous people in it?

Far be it from you to do such a thing—to kill the righteous with the wicked, treating the righteous and the wicked alike. Far be it from you! Will not the Judge of all the earth do right?"

The LORD said, "If I find fifty righteous people in the city of Sodom, I will spare the whole place for their sake."

Then Abraham spoke up again: "Now that I have been so bold as to speak to the Lord, though I am nothing but dust and ashes,

what if the number of the righteous is five less than fifty? Will you destroy the whole city for lack of five people?" "If I find forty-five there," he said, "I will not destroy it."

Once again he spoke to him, "What if only forty are found there?" He said, "For the sake of forty, I will not do it."

Then he said, "May the Lord not be angry, but let me speak. What if only thirty can be found there?" He answered, "I will not do it if I find thirty there."

Abraham said, "Now that I have been so bold as to speak to the Lord, what if only twenty can be found there?" He said, "For the sake of twenty, I will not destroy it."

Then he said, "May the Lord not be angry, but let me speak just once more. What if only ten can be found there?" He answered, "For the sake of ten, I will not destroy it."

When the LORD had finished speaking with Abraham, he left, and Abraham returned home.

The people of Sodom were not just grievously sinning, but they were forcing their sinful ways onto others around them such that the cries of the neighboring people reached heaven! For example, they even wanted to force their sexual immorality onto Lot's visitors, the angels, so they must have been forcing themselves onto their neighbors in many ways—political, business, morality, and other ways—for them to cry to heaven for help!

Sodom and Gomorrah were infamous cities of the time. We do not know the population; perhaps there were around one thousand in each city. Abraham pressed in on God's character of justice to spare Sodom if only just ten were found to be righteous. What we later find is only the household of Lot was considered righteous, less than ten people, so angels spared them by bringing them out of the city. Unfortunately, the children of the cities had been corrupted by their parents, and the Righteous Judge did not want them to grow up to live their lives as their parents were living theirs, so He took them to the safety of His heaven.

For the sake of just ten, perhaps just 1 percent of the population, the Lord was willing to stay judgment! That is extremely merciful; no one can accuse God of not being merciful, ever. If they do, they are just trying to rationalize their own sinful behavior. (Remember, mercy is not getting what we deserve; Grace is getting what we don't deserve.)

In Jude 7–8 (Good News Translation) we are told what the other specific sins of Sodom were:

> *Remember Sodom and Gomorrah, and the nearby towns, whose people acted as those angels did and indulged in sexual immorality and perversion: they suffer the punishment of eternal fire as a plain warning to all. In the same way also, these people have visions which make them sin against their own bodies; they despise God's authority and insult the glorious beings above.*

Three specific sins are cited; the people of Sodom acted as those fallen angels had:

1. Indulging in sexual immorality and perversion. The Greek definition of the word in the text, "fornication," means to commit illicit sexual intercourse. Illicit would be other than between a husband and his wife. Sexual perversion would be broader, including bestiality, and other perversions of God's gift of sexuality (Jude 7 GNT).
2. The people of Sodom, like the fallen angels, despised God's authority (Jude 8 GNT).
3. Insulting heavenly beings. Jude 8 (GNT), which means insulting, mocking even the wonderful heavenly things God created. The following verses expound on these sins through history and the consequences those people suffered being similar to Sodom. So, one of the purposes of the destruction of a whole group of sinful people was as an object lesson to Abraham's descendants to obey God not their own evil desires (Genesis 18:19 GNT).

The people of Sodom are described this way in Jude 14–16 (GNT):

It was Enoch, the seventh[b] direct descendant from Adam, who long ago prophesied this about them: "The Lord will come with many thousands of his holy angels to bring judgment on all, to condemn them all for the godless deeds they have performed and for all the terrible words that godless sinners have spoken against him!" These people are always grumbling and blaming others; they follow their own evil desires. They brag about themselves and flatter others in order to get their own way.

For these sins, God sent His judgment of fire onto the cities. It is of interest to note that Sumerian astronomers (great-grandfathers of the magi who brought gifts to baby Jesus) noted in their clay tablets an asteroid coming in at a low angle, breaking up (possibly hitting the top of the Alps to assist it in breaking up) and landing in numerous balls of fire in the vicinity of these cities at about this time. Today there is a layer of ash below the ground where these cities existed. So, they had been destroyed by fire. We know an object entering earth's atmosphere burns red hot and can break into many pieces.

The neighboring peoples around Sodom were crying out to God because the people of Sodom and Gomorrah must have been imposing their evil ways on them just as they wanted to impose their selfish power and aggression in a gang rape onto the visiting angels at Lot's house. The Lord heard the cries of Sodom's neighbors, so to protect them and prevent them from being influenced to adopt Sodom's evil practices, He destroyed the cities. As the Creator of everything, the Righteous Judge has the divine right to destroy evil how and when He sees fit. He does not need our permission or approval.

God hates it when men use their power to impose injustice on other men (Amos 5:10 NIV).

There are those who oppress the innocent and take bribes

*and deprive the poor of justice in the courts. (Amos
5:12 NIV)*

But let justice roll on like a river,

*righteousness like a never-failing stream! (Amos
5:24 NIV)*

Dr. Martin Luther King often quoted these eternal words.

So, the parents of Sodom and future empires were judged for their sins, their moral depravity, teaching their children to be likewise, and violating the freedom of their neighbors by forcing their sinful conduct onto them, who cried out to the Lord to stop it. The parents were destroyed in the fire and brimstone, and their souls went to Eternal Judgment.

God also took the physical lives of the children of Sodom along with the adults, so the children could be spared the judgment of their eternal spirits. I would not be surprised if the souls of the children were taken just moments before the brimstone hit, so the parents knew they were doubly judged, by the eternal God taking the souls of the children away from them. They would enter a new life in paradise (as Jesus said to the repentant sinner dying on the cross next to Him, today you will be with me in Paradise!) sitting with Jesus teaching them the right way to live and love. He would teach them the two greatest commandments—to love God with all their hearts, minds, souls, and strength—and the second like unto it—to love their neighbors as themselves. Totally opposite of what their parents had taught them. The Righteous Judge hates sinful lifestyles, disobedience to His authority, and forcing your evil ways onto others, violating the freedoms and God given-right of liberty to others.

What is Jesus's response to adults corrupting children?

*¹At that time the disciples came to Jesus and asked,
"Who then is the greatest in the kingdom of heaven?"
²Jesus invited a little child to stand among them.*

³"Truly I tell you," He said, "unless you change and become like little children, you will never enter the kingdom of heaven. ⁴Therefore, whoever humbles himself like this little child is the greatest in the kingdom of heaven. ⁵And whoever welcomes a little child like this in My name welcomes Me. ⁶But if anyone causes one of these little ones who believe in Me to stumble, it would be better for him to have a large millstone hung around his neck and to be drowned in the depths of the sea. (Matthew 18:1–6 Berean Study Bible)

Jesus further said in Matthew 18:⁷ Woe to the world because of the things that cause people to stumble! Such things must come, but woe to the person through whom they come! ⁸If your hand or your foot causes you to stumble cut it off and throw it away. It is better for you to enter life maimed or crippled than to have two hands or two feet and be thrown into eternal fire. ⁹And if your eye causes you to stumble, gouge it out and throw it away. It is better for you to enter life with one eye than to have two eyes and be thrown into the fire of hell. (NIV)

What was the consequence of a generation of children in Nazi Germany, Imperial Japan, and Communist Russia being indoctrinated by their parents, schools, and governments into growing up believing they had a right to inflict their will and their godless ideology upon their neighbors, using their free will to ignore God and His Love? The result was the world suffered the loss of sixty-eight million people in World War II, because too many of the sons and daughters of Germany, Japan, and Russia grew up believing they could force their will and ideology onto their neighbors. For fifty years after World War II, hundreds of millions more were murdered and enslaved to communism.

So, let's not blame God for the moral, political, racial, and other evils on this planet. It is caused by zealous, misguided ideologues misusing their God-given free will to enslave other men and women, boys and girls, stripping away their freedom and forcing them to submit to their ideological and political agenda. Instead, the God of our fathers, the

Author of Liberty, calls upon us to use our free will to lose the chains of injustice and iniquity and to promote liberty and justice for all.

"America"

Our fathers' God to Thee,
Author of liberty,
To Thee we sing.
Long may our land be bright,
With freedom's holy light,
Protect us by Thy might,
Great God our King.
What we teach our children today, will affect the kind of world we will live in tomorrow.

Epilogue

We hope the answers to these difficult life questions has brought the reader into a deeper understanding of the character and person of our Creator so that a closer relationship with Him is sought.

Jesus said, "Behold, I stand at the door and knock. If anyone hears My voice and opens the door, I will come in to him and dine with him, and he with Me" (Revelation 3:20 NASB).

Will you open the door of your heart to Jesus today?

Bob Green

Notes

Notes

Printed in the United States
by Baker & Taylor Publisher Services